# WHY?

A cat's acrobatics, the tricks mirrors play on you, and balloon-shaped bubbles are all explained in *WHY?*

If you have ever wondered which animal runs the fastest, *WHY?* will tell you. Or maybe jet engines and sound waves are real puzzlers. In that case, *WHY?* has the answers.

The odd and strange things that happen to you, such as the feeling you get riding in an elevator or the goosebumps on your skin, are things you have always known about but not known why.

Find out why in this fascinating book of questions and answers.

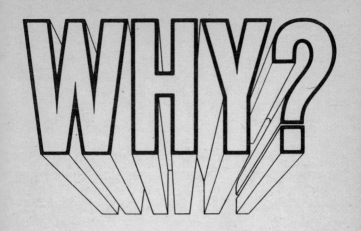

# WHY?

**Eric Laithwaite**
**Illustrated by Mike Jackson**

**Watermill Press**
Mahwah, New Jersey

Published by: **Watermill Press**
          **Mahwah, N.J.**

ISBN 0-8167-1683-8

Copyright © 1989 Kidsbooks, Inc.

Manufactured in the United States of America

# Contents

Why does a glowworm glow? 10
How does a bat "see" in the dark? 12
How does a cat land on its feet when
   it falls? 14
How does soap clean? 19
What is the Milky Way? 20
Why do you sink in quicksand? 22
How can you start yourself on a swing
   without touching the ground? 24
How does Newton's cradle work? 26
Why does your hair crackle when it is
   combed? 28
Can your eyes play tricks on you? 31

Do sound waves ever die out?                              35
When the light is turned off at night, you
    cannot see at first. Why is this?                     36
What makes the rain *rain*?                               38
Why do you feel funny inside when you
    think you are falling?                                40
Does a light bulb last longer when you
    switch it on and off, or keep it burning?             42
What causes lightning?                                    44
What makes you get goosebumps?                            47
Do all the moths you see flying around
    really eat wool?                                      48
If a queen bee dies, how do the bees in
    the hive produce a new queen?                         50
Why is a bad habit so hard to break?                      52

What is symmetry? 54
How can we catch the sun's energy? 56
Which animal runs the fastest? 58
When you look into a mirror, your left hand becomes your right hand, so why doesn't your head become your feet? 60
Can you tell what someone is saying without hearing them? 63
How high are the clouds? 64
How are velvet and satin made? 66
How do you make concrete? 68
How do you draw an ellipse? 70
Why can't you blow square bubbles? 72

Why does a faucet drip?     74

What happens in an eclipse?     76

How does a fire extinguisher work?     78

Why does a heap of grass cuttings get
hot in the middle?     80

How can a wine glass be broken by a
musical note?     82

How does a jet engine work?     84

Why do old trains go clickety-clack?     86

Does the earth have a crust?     88

Is a comet a shooting star?     90

Why does metal feel so cold in the
winter and so hot in summer?     92

What makes a sonic boom?     94

# Why does a glowworm glow?

A glowworm is not a worm at all, but a female beetle. Nor is a firefly a fly. It, too, is a beetle, and it also glows, or flickers.

A wingless female glowworm must attract males to fertilize the eggs she lays. She makes the rear end of her body glow in the dark. The male can see the light and recognize it as coming from a female glowworm. The eggs of this beetle glow a little.

Fireflies glow to attract mates, too, but in fireflies the males also glow.

There are several interesting facts about the glow. It is a "cold" light — unlike the familiar "hot" light from an electric light bulb. Yet it is different from manufactured cold lights, such as phosphorescent paints used on the figures and faces of watches and clocks so that we can tell time in the dark.

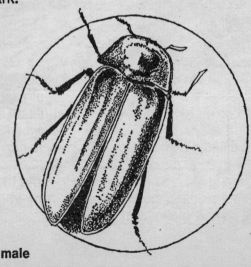

10    male

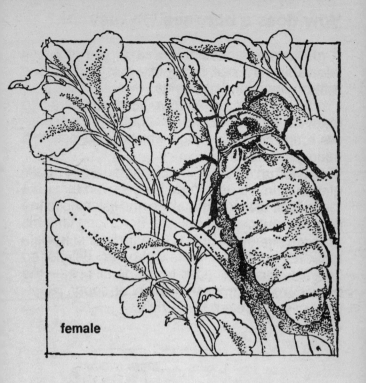

**female**

Scientists cannot completely explain the light of a glowworm's glow, or how fireflies sometimes flicker all at the same time. It is usually easier to see a faint light a long way off if it goes on and off than if it stays on all the time. Glowworms glow and fireflies flicker to make it easier to communicate with their mates.

So we know some of the *whys* about the glow of these beetles, but we really know very little about *how* a glowworm glows.

# How does a bat "see" in the dark?

If you have ever been in a cave, you probably know that bats can fly rapidly in total darkness without bumping into things.

How is this possible? Two hundred years ago many scientists believed that bats had very sensitive tips on their wings which could detect a nearby object.

In 1799 an Italian scientist named Spellanzani came up with a new idea. He believed that bats found their way by squeaking and listening to the echoes bouncing off objects. For a long time his work was ignored. But, 120 years later scientists repeated his experiments when they developed an echo depth sounder for ships at sea — the device we call acoustic radar, or *sonar*. Spellanzani was proven to be right.

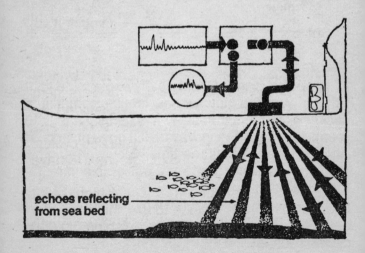

echoes reflecting from sea bed

The squeaks of a bat are measured in cycles/second, or cycles per second. Our ears hear sounds of up to about 15,000 cycles/second. To give an idea how high 15,000 cycles/second are, just think that middle C on a piano is 256 cycles/second, the C above it 512, the next octave 1,024, and so on.

15,000 cycles/second may seem high, but it does not even come close to the shrillness of a bat's squeak which is an astonishing 50,000 cycles/second!

# How does a cat land on its feet when it falls?

Have you ever watched a cat fall from a table or high shelf? Even if it starts to fall with its back to the floor, it almost always lands on its feet.

We might think that the cat should continue to fall in its starting position. But cats have flexible bodies which move easily. Just like acrobats, they sail through the air and land safely and gracefully.

If you watched a slow-motion movie you could see that the cat twists the front and back parts of its body so that its feet point downward. But, how does the cat manage to do this in free flight?

When a cat falls, it first pulls in its front legs and sticks out its back legs and tail. Almost at the same time it twists. The cat's front end turns sharply, and the back end only slightly. Then it throws out its front legs, puts its tail straight out, and manages to twist its back end. This happens so quickly that your eye almost misses these movements. Next, it arches its back and seems to "float" like a parachute to the floor, feet first.

The cat's twist is like an extra boost. Each twist kicks off an additional one. The cat's "waist," or middle section, acts like a pivot. The front end and back end of the cat's body can turn at different times. Finally, each part of the cat's body is feet down, and it falls safely.

# How does soap clean?

Liquids, like all other substances, are made up of *molecules.* One molecule of water is the smallest amount of water that has all the special qualities of water.

Imagine that you and some friends are molecules of water. Hold hands tightly and form a chain. If another friend tries to break through your locked hands, he or she will probably find it rather difficult. When molecules of water stick together, a "skin" forms on the surface. This is called surface tension.

Now, imagine that everyone in the chain linked pinkies. It would be easy for your friend to break the barrier. Some substances can break down the surface tension of water, making the links less strong, like the pinkies' bonds. Soap is one substance that can do this.

Washing clothes in plain water will not really clean them because water's surface tension keeps the tiny dirt particles out. Since soap breaks up this skin, the dirt can be loosened from clothes, enter the water more easily, and leave clothes clean.

# What is the Milky Way?

Look at the night sky and you can see hundreds upon hundreds of stars. What you see as a star may be one of many things. A star can be like our own fiery sun and may have planets circling around it. But, because it is so far away it seems to be no larger than a pinhead, and its planets cannot be seen at all. Sometimes it is not really a star, but a planet reflecting the rays of the sun, like the planet Venus which we call the Morning Star. We may also see a hazy spot which is really a huge cloud of stars. This collection of stars is a galaxy. Astronomers with powerful telescopes can study distant galaxies we cannot even see.

Some galaxies are shaped liked gigantic wheels. Our galaxy is wheel shaped, and our sun

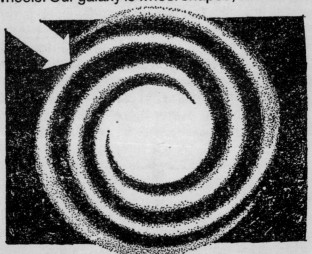

**our galaxy — position of the sun shown by arrow**

is close to the edge. That is why when we look in one direction we can see many more stars than in any other part of the sky. (Imagine looking toward the hub from the edge of the wheel.) We see nearer suns as stars against a background of "milkiness" made by the millions of stars in the hub of the wheel and beyond. This white area in the sky is long and narrow and looks like a path or way, so it is called the Milky Way. Its light is very much like the whiteness of a heavy snowfall. If you look at the Milky Way through binoculars, the haziness disappears and thousands of stars appear as bright as snowflakes.

# Why do you sink in quicksand?

When a solid object, such as wood, is placed in a liquid, such as water, it will float if its density is less than the density of water. If it sinks, it is more dense, or heavier. If an object is made of many things, such as a bag of wood, metal, plastic, etc., whether it floats or sinks depends upon its *average density.*

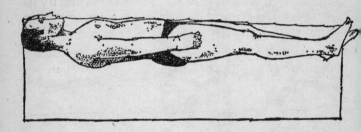

It is a strange coincidence that the average density of the human body is very, very slightly less than the density of water. The difference is so small that if you were to remain still when in deep water and keep your body vertical, as when standing on land, you would drown because your mouth and nose would be under water and you could not breathe. Only the top of your head would be above the water level. If you wish to float remaining perfectly still, you must get yourself into an almost horizontal position so that just the front of your face is out of the water. Floating is much easier if you move — flutter your legs and extend your arms outward, sometimes "rowing" yourself through the water.

Quicksand looks like solid sand, but it's not. It is a mixture of water and sand, and acts more like a liquid than a solid. Water fills the spaces between the roughly-shaped grains of sand which touch each other in only a few places. Quicksand looks solid, so people run or walk onto it without realizing at first that they are beginning to sink.

It is possible to float in quicksand, but no one would want to. It is best to avoid it. People caught in quicksand should not panic. They should try to bend their knees and lie on their backs, imitating a floating position in water. If they are confident enough to relax their legs, they will rise again until their whole body floats.

# How can you start yourself on a swing without touching the ground?

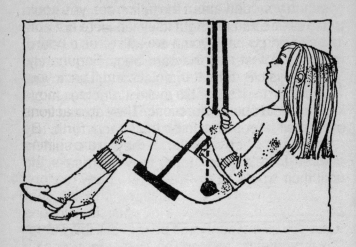

If you hop on a high swing and there is no one to give a push, you have to start yourself without touching the ground.

When you read about the falling cat, you could see how it could not right itself if it were not able to bend and twist. If you were as stiff as a board, you would never be able to swing. Fortunately, your body is flexible, too. You can pull back your body from the waist. This makes your legs move out in the opposite direction. These two actions cause a little movement back and forth. By grasping and releasing the ropes you are shifting your weight; that helps too. You can make the swinging bigger by reversing your body motions — bending your legs inward and bringing your back forward. These sets of opposite motions keep you swinging. Some people call this pumping. If you want to stop the swinging, you also have to stop the pumping motion until you slow to a standstill.

# How does Newton's cradle work?

Newton's cradle is made of steel balls hanging by fine threads from a frame. They are positioned so that they just touch each other.

Pull back the ball at one end of the row, and let it go. When it hits the other balls the ball at the opposite end shoots out at what seems to be the same instant.

In a five ball cradle, two balls can be pulled aside, let go, and then two shoot out from the other end. However, you may think it strange when three balls out of five are moved and cause three balls to bounce at the other end. And even stranger when four balls cause four to swing. It does not seem possible that some of the original balls pulled out should also shoot out.

You can begin to understand how the cradle works by thinking about a croquet game. You may have two balls, A and B, touching each other. By pressing your foot on A and smacking it with a mallet, you can make B move. This is because the force of the mallet stroke travels through A and hits B which is free to move.

A similar thing happens in the cradle. When the first ball is pulled, it quickly transfers its energy of motion through the other balls to move the last in such a small fraction of a second that you think the two balls move at the same time.

If you were able to take the cradle apart, reposition the balls, and make a few experiments with the balls farther apart and *not* touching, you would see that if you start with enough moving energy for three balls, you will keep three moving. And if there is energy for four balls, you keep four moving. When the balls touch, of course, the energy is transferred immediately.

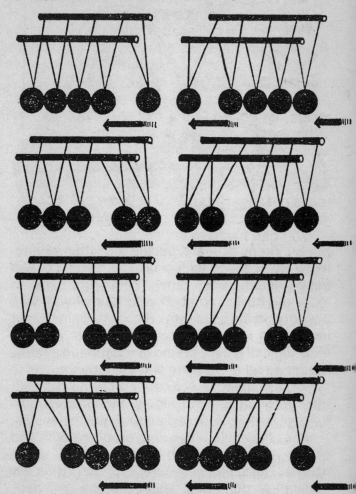

# Why does your hair crackle when it is combed?

For hundreds of years, people thought that electricity was caused by friction, the rubbing of two things against each other. You might think so too, from having combed your hair when it was very dry. In the sixteenth century William Gilbert impressed Queen Elizabeth with this idea by showing that a certain kind of rod rubbed against cat fur could attract tiny pieces of paper.

But, electricity is not caused by the rubbing. First you may think of atoms, the smallest particles of matter. You read about water molecules. A water molecule has two hydrogen atoms and one oxygen atom. Each atom has a ball in the middle. This ball is called the *nucleus*. Inside the nucleus are tiny bits called *protons* and *neu-*

*trons.* The nucleus is surrounded by even smaller bits, *electrons,* which go around it in circular paths. The illustration shows the paths of electrons in one atom.

When two substances come into contact, some of the electrons of one substance gather on the other. The larger the area of contact, the greater chance there is for an exchange of electrons. The more electrons a substance collects, the more charged it becomes.

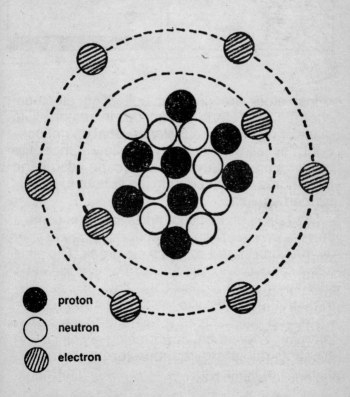

● proton

○ neutron

◍ electron

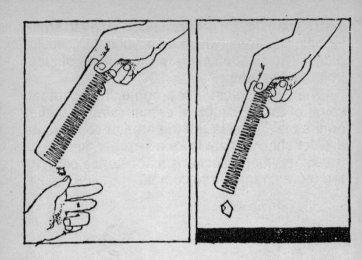

Insulators are good at collecting electrical charges and storing them up. Insulators, like glass or plastic, are substances that do not conduct, or allow electricity to flow. Once the charges are in, they cannot escape even if the insulator is separated from the substance it was rubbed against.

Dry hair is an insulator and when you comb it there is an exchange of electrons because your dry hair has stored so many electrons. The air is a fair conductor of electricity. The crackles and little sparks are signs of the flow of electricity through the air, just like the tiny jolts you receive when you walk across a rug and touch something like a doorknob. So, combing dry hair is like creating miniature thunderstorms with their charges of lightning.

# Can your eyes play tricks on you?

Take a look at the picture. Which "picture" did you see first? Did you see a candlestick, or did you see two people? Often you look at the objects in a picture in a certain way, forgetting what the space between them looks like.

Your eyes are wonderful instruments that help you see light, shadow, pattern and color. But sometimes they do strange things to you.

The eye is very much like a camera. It takes a picture through a lens. In a fraction of a second the picture is "developed" by the brain, which tells you what you are seeing. The eye is constantly taking pictures. When you watch TV or a movie, you do not realize you are seeing one little picture followed by another, and another. (It really is that way on film.) What is happening is called *persistence of vision,* or, in less fancy terms, the brain stores a picture during the tiny parts of a second between each picture. So, you

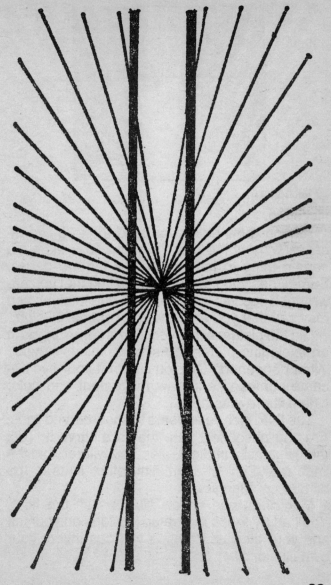

33

see smoothly, and you are not aware of any flickering.

As you grow older, you tend to store experiences without too much thought. You expect a certain thing to happen from a familiar cause. Sometimes you are surprised to find that you are wrong! If such an experience is due to sight, you may say that you are having an *optical illusion*.

Did the picture of the very fine lines arranged in an exploding pattern do strange things to you? What happened? Did you find that your eye became confused and saw movement and color where there was none?

The third picture appears to show curved lines. Are you absolutely sure they are curved? Test them against a straight ruler. You will see that the lines really are straight. The other lines in the picture confuse you.

Magicians use optical illusions all the time. You can try these illustrated illusions on yourself and your friends. Perhaps you can invent your own illusions.

34

# Do sound waves ever die out?

When you speak, clap hands, or close a book you make sound. Sound moves through the air in waves.

You can see what sound waves are like if you drop a pebble in a smooth pond. Ripples form around the spot where the pebble fell. At first the ripples are small circles. You can see them easily. Then they grow. The larger the circles become, the harder the waves are to see. If the pond had no end, the ripples would just become fainter and fainter before they finally disappeared, slowed down by the friction of water molecules.

Sound waves move in the air like ripples getting fainter and finally disappearing as they are farther away from their source.

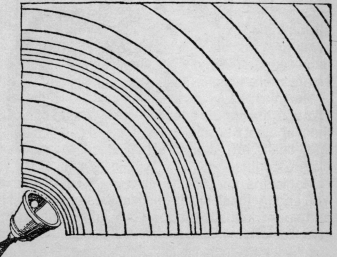

# When the light is turned off at night, you cannot see at first. Why is this?

You know that your eyes can trick you with optical illusions. In normal situations your eyes see quickly and efficiently. However, when lighting changes rapidly, your eyes can do more strange things.

Enter a dark cellar from bright daylight. Your eyes react slowly as they try to adjust to the absence of light.

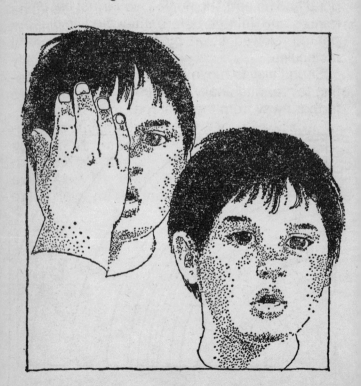

Then after getting used to the dark, go outside. It will be a long time before you stop squinting and wrinkling your face.

Light enters your eyes through the pupil (the black hole in the middle of the eye). The size of the pupil is shaped by the iris (the colored part). The iris is like a ring. The thicker the ring, the more tightly it closes around the pupil so that a small amount of light enters the eye. It does this in bright light. The thinner the ring, the bigger the pupil, so that a larger amount of light enters the eye. It does this in dim light. Your iris cannot be controlled at will. Its movement is *involuntary*. When you go quickly from light to dark, or dark to light, your iris cannot open or close quickly enough to help you adjust. So, it is several seconds or maybe even a minute before you are comfortable.

Another interesting fact about irises — although we cannot voluntarily control the opening and closing of our irises, cats can. Perhaps you may see how a cat opens its irises if you move a small object near it when its extra eyelids are nearly closed.

# What makes the rain *rain*?

Raindrops fall from clouds, and showers sprinkle us with a mist of dampness. Rain is such an everyday happening.

Have you ever wondered what makes the rain *rain*? What makes a raindrop form and fall from a cloud, and how does it get there in the first place?

Think about a boiling pot of water, or your breath on a cold morning. The steam you see is really water vapor — lots of water molecules that have escaped into the air.

Water vapor rises from the surface of lakes, rivers, and oceans, too. This *evaporation* is taking place all of the time. When millions and millions of water vapor molecules are brought into contact with cool air, clouds are formed.

Only under certain conditions will the water vapor of clouds *condense,* or collect into droplets of rain. This will happen if the water vapor

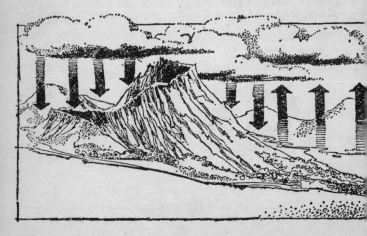

is chilled enough. Think of the dew on grass on a chilly morning. Just about the same thing happens within a cloud, and its droplets of water fall as raindrops.

If a water molecule has something it can hang onto, it will form a droplet of rain much more easily. The tiniest particle of dust is enough to produce a raindrop high in the air. It is the dirt particles which make clouds look so dark. If you catch rain water in a jar and let it stand for a few hours, you will see a collection of dirt at the bottom which was only hours ago a black cloud!

It is possible to make the rain *rain* by flying an airplane above the clouds and dropping chemicals. They can lower the temperature of the water vapor and give the water molecules particles to hang onto.

When it rains, more water is added to lakes, rivers, and oceans. Some of that water will evaporate, new clouds will form, and the whole rain cycle will begin again.

# Why do you feel funny inside when you think you are falling?

*Star Wars* has given you the popular expression "May the force be with you." One force that is always with you is the force of gravity.

You get a funny feeling when you slip, or jump from a high wall, or ride a car over a bumpy road or hump-backed bridge. This is because your speed of motion is *accelerating,* or becoming much faster, and for a moment, as you fall, you feel weightless. You feel strange when you start to go up or down in an elevator. Once the elevator begins to move steadily, you feel fine because you do not feel any different than you do when you are standing still.

Your stomach can get queasy if you accelerate upward, as in an airplane or an elevator. But you seem to notice the pressure on your feet more than the strange feeling in your stomach. This probably dates back to the time when our ancestors lived in trees. Climbing was usual. Falling, though, could be dangerous. Falling for most people is more alarming than rising.

Astronauts in outer space have to be trained to get used to being weightless because there is no gravity in outer space.

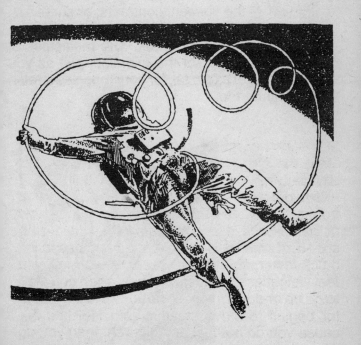

# Does a light bulb last longer when you switch it on and off, or keep it burning?

Electric light bulbs with filaments give out light because the electricity running through the bulb causes its filament to heat up and glow. The filament is the thread-like wire inside the bulb. It does not burn out immediately because there is no oxygen within the bulb to allow it to burn, and oxygen is needed to make things burn.

Switch a light on — the sudden rise in temperature expands, or stretches, the filament. Switch a light off — the filament contracts, or shrinks. A metal that is always being expanded and contracted will eventually break. The molecules of filament "get tired" of the exercise, just as you tire after lots of exercise, for your muscles stretch and contract too.

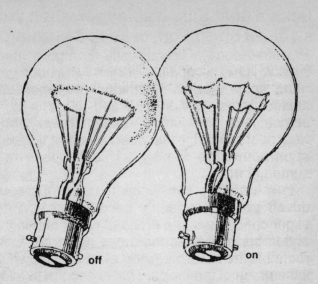

off      on

Picture two rooms, each with a light bulb. Imagine that you leave one light burning for a certain amount of time, and flick the other one on and off during the same period of time. If you did this experiment you would find that the bulb that was switched would burn out first, even though it was not on constantly, because its filament was strained.

Another problem with a light bulb can happen if you change its position, or simply take it from its socket to clean it. When you do this, the chances are that the bulb will burn out soon. This happens because the filament has been strained; it is brittle and fragile and should not be moved. So, be careful with your electric light bulbs. Only use them when necessary, and don't flick them on and off.

# What causes lightning?

Electrical current flows easily through a metal wire, which is a good conductor. Air is not a very good conductor of electricity, but when you shuffle across a wool rug and touch a metal object, electricity "jumps" through the air, and it "leaps" through the air when a bolt of lightning streaks through the sky. This happens in a thunderstorm.

In a violent storm warm masses of air are driven up and suddenly become cold. Water vapor condenses into drops of water and larger and larger drops. As the drops get larger there are more and more circling electrons crowding the surface of the drops. That is enough to allow an electric current to suddenly streak down from the clouds and hit the earth.

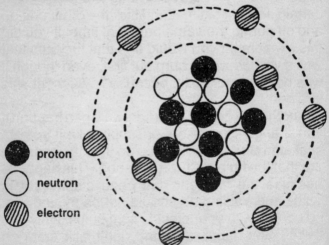

- ● proton
- ○ neutron
- ◐ electron

one of the atoms in a water molecule with its electrons circling

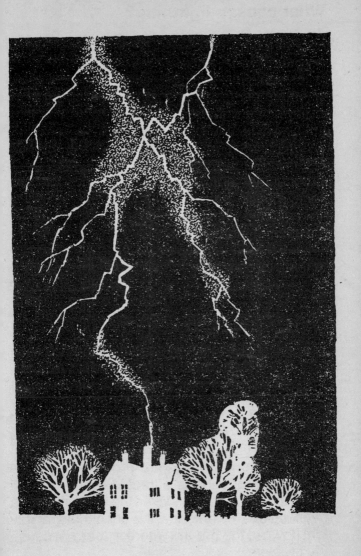

Once the lightning starts, one bolt follows another. Lightning builds up rapidly. It is like lined up dominoes. One domino falling triggers all the others to topple.

The electricity flow in a lightning bolt is much greater than currents supplied by power companies, but it only lasts a fraction of a second. Such large currents produce huge amounts of heat and are like an explosion.

Thunder is the sound of the explosion caused by lightning. The sight of lightning reaches us immediately. The sound of thunder follows a few seconds later. By counting the time in seconds between seeing lightning and hearing thunder you can roughly figure out how many miles away the stroke of lightning hit — about one thousand feet for every second, or one mile every five seconds.

Buildings and houses are protected by lightning rods. Lightning is attracted to the highest things around. When it strikes the lightning rod, a metal rod or a TV antenna, it is conducted rapidly right down to the ground where it does not cause any problem.

# What makes you get goosebumps?

Certainly you have noticed how bumpy the skin on your arms and legs becomes when you are cold. You call these tiny lumps goosebumps. They pop up without any thought on your part. Your body is trying to make its hairs stand straight out from the skin.

Why should your body do this? The hairs standing out can trap a layer of air around your body and help keep you warm. Our much hairier ancestors warmed themselves this way. Today we lack the hair, but we still have bumps.

Furry animals such as cats make their hair stand up not only when they are cold, but when they are frightened or being aggressive. Watch how a cat swells up when a dog comes near. Its bristly hair makes it look larger and perhaps scarier to its enemy.

## Do all the moths you see flying around really eat wool?

Most people have two mistaken ideas about clothes moths. First, it is not the moth that does the eating — it is its caterpillar. A caterpillar has jaws for biting, but an adult moth only has a tube through which it sucks fluids. Second, of the many kinds of moth, only a very few kinds attack clothes in the caterpillar stage. Many people seeing the large brown moths that come to lighted windows, imagine that the creatures are trying to get in to lay eggs on their clothes. But this is not so.

Scientists know for certain that the kind of moth whose caterpillar eats clothes lived in prehistoric times when people lived in caves. But so did animals that were covered with wool. So, of course the caterpillars fed on animals' wool.

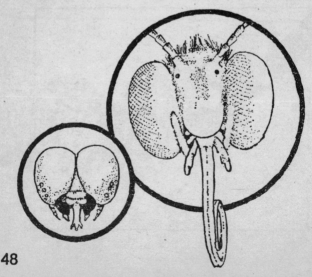

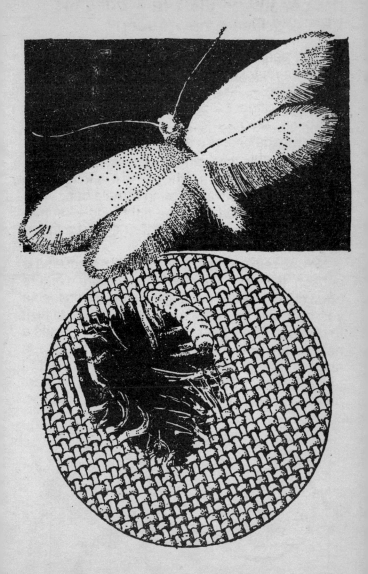

# If a queen bee dies, how does the hive produce a new queen?

Every beehive is an organized little world. It is ruled by a queen bee. She is served by females called workers. Males called drones also live in the hive.

The queen bee is larger than all the other bees. Also, she is the one fertile female, that is, the only female that can lay eggs. When a queen bee dies, the workers, whose job it is to feed the young, select a strong, young female bee. Then they begin feeding it on the right food — sometimes called bee-jelly — so that it grows into a large and perfect female.

No one really knows just how the new queen is chosen. It is very likely that one or more workers often create new queens. If the workers do feed a young queen, the reigning queen will try to sting it to death before it becomes strong. Sometimes a new queen and a few loyal workers do escape and form a new beehive. It is very important that this happens. Without new hives being formed, the bees could become extinct, that is, die out.

queen

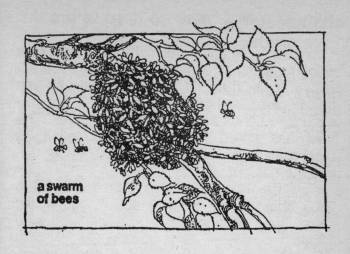

a swarm
of bees

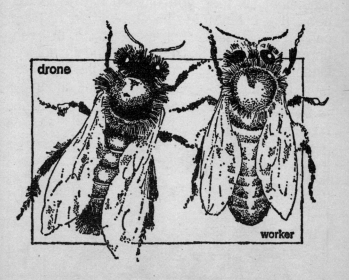

drone

worker

# Why is a bad habit so hard to break?

There are many things you can do over and over without having to think about them. These actions are called habits. Walking is easy for you now because you don't have to think about how each joint bends and each muscle moves. The brain has stored the "how-to" information, so that you can walk automatically. You have gotten into the habit of walking.

Habits make life easier for you. If you had to think about every ordinary action, you would never have time to play, read, or learn new things.

Some habits are not useful. If, for example, you bite your nails because you are worried, that is one thing. But when you bite your nails for no reason at all, then you have a bad nailbiting habit. It is important to break bad habits. They can be unpleasant, such as nailbiting, or even harmful such as cigarette smoking in adults. Changing habits is difficult because the brain has stored the habit. So, you have to think and think

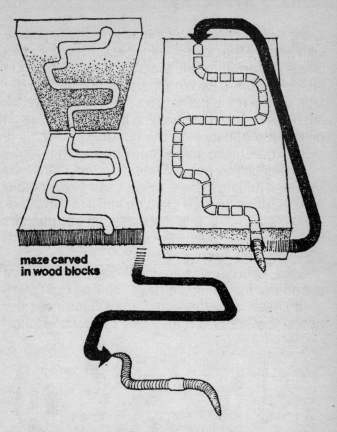

maze carved
in wood blocks

some more to remove the habit that is locked into the automatic part of your brain.

Animals, birds and insects form habits, too. You can "teach" a worm to go through a maze. Let it travel through the maze many times. Later, when it is placed on a bare table, it will repeat the maze pattern. The worm has learned a habit.

# What is symmetry?

Have you ever tried to make a snowflake design with paper? It is not as difficult as it seems. Fold a piece of paper in half. Snip designs of different shapes into the paper. Open the paper. The design on the right appears on the left, or, depending upon how you are holding the paper, a design on the top appears on the bottom.

You can make even more interesting snowflake designs by using a square or circular piece of paper, folding it once, twice, even three, or four times. But make sure that you fold it in a *symmetrical* way, that is, fold the circle right through its middle. Fold it again so that the edges match perfectly and keep on going.

Solid, or three-dimensional objects can have symmetry too. Animals have left and right symmetry. Generally there are small differences between the left and right sides of any one parti-

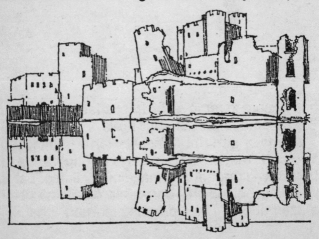

cular animal. We make differences in right and left symmetry by parting our hair on one side or another, for example.

On the outside of your body, eyes, ears, arms, legs form a left-right symmetry. However, if you could look at the inside of your body, at organs such as the stomach or heart, you would see that it is not completely symmetrical. The outside of a car is almost perfectly symmetrical, right and left, but the engine on the inside is not.

The most common up and down symmetry in nature can be seen reflected in a pool of water. Very calm lakes mirror mountains or buildings near the water's edge.

Symmetry is very important in designs and in engineering. Think of the design of a bicycle with its front wheel and back wheel, its right and left handlebars. Without symmetry you would not be able to ride your bicycle!

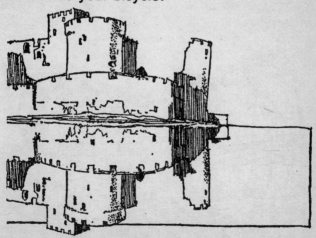

# How can we catch the sun's energy?

Most of the heat energy we use has come from the sun. When you hang laundry on a clothesline, the heat of the sun dries your clothes. It bakes adobe bricks to make houses with in the southwest. Coal dug from the earth is the remains of forests that grew millions of years ago. The plants of those forests got their energy from the sun. Coal has been storing it for a long time.

It is very important that we know how to use solar, or sun, energy wisely because there are limited supplies of oil and coal, the most used heating materials. People are now trying harder than ever to catch the energy of the sun to heat homes and other buildings. One way that people

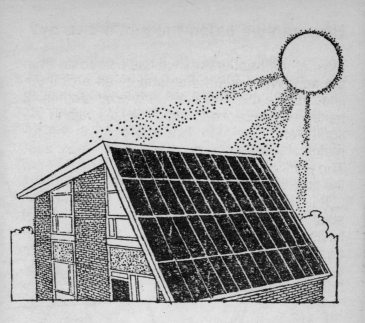

can heat their homes with solar energy is by making a greenhouse type of heat trap. Large metal sheets under sheets of glass are placed on rooftops; the sun heats the metal; and the heat is trapped.

Other ways of saving the sun's energy are with solar cells, like storage batteries. There are also mirrors that focus and collect heat. Scientists, inventors, and designers are trying to invent new ways to harness the sun's energy. We have barely scratched the surface of knowing all there is to know about the sun's energy and how to capture it and save it.

# Which animal runs the fastest?

No one really knows whether the fastest speed at any instant has ever been recorded correctly for any animal. But here are some comparisons:

A cheetah is supposed to be the fastest land animal. In a short burst of speed it can reach 60 miles per hour.

Race horses gallop at about 40 miles per hour.

A well trained athlete can run a little more than half a mile in about 2½ minutes, which is about 15 miles per hour. The record speed for a mile is

just under four minutes, or about 12 miles per hour. A marathon runner covers the 26-mile 385-yard distance of that race at about 7½ to 8 miles per hour.

Some animals are fast in special ways. Antelope develop a great deal of speed due to their ability to make long leaps. Birds can fly faster than land animals can run. One bird, the swift, can reach a speed of about 87 miles per hour. Even the snail is not the slowest of animals. The snail *can* move about a yard a minute. Believe it or not, it can beat some of its fellow creatures at that speed.

# When you look into a mirror, your left hand becomes your right hand, so why doesn't your head become your feet?

Try this experiment. Place a mirror on a table. Look into it and write an R where your right hand is reflected and an L where the left hand appears. Now walk around to the back of the mirror. Write an R for the right side and an L for your left side. If you compare each side of the mirror, right is left and left is right.

Now stand in front of a floor-length mirror and move your left leg. Your mirror image moves too, only the mirror "person's" right leg moves. That

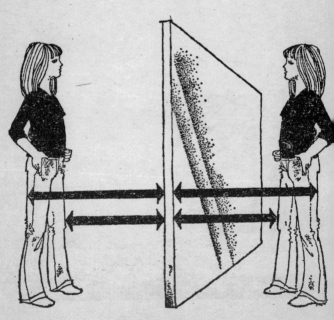

is, if you were standing at the mirror's surface, or, if you were that "person" the leg that moved would be your right leg.

Since a mirror reverses right and left, why doesn't it turn you upside down too? The reason is that a mirror produces an image every part of which is as far behind the reflecting surface as the part of the object — your leg, for instance — is in front of it. It is the distance from the

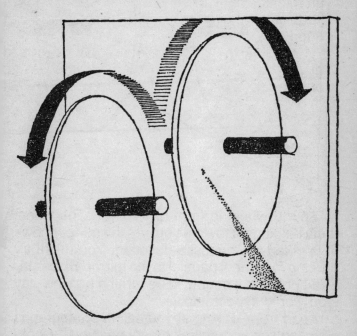

mirror's surface that makes the image — in this case your leg's action — in the mirror. The switch or reversal, you see in a mirror's image is only of sides, not up and down.

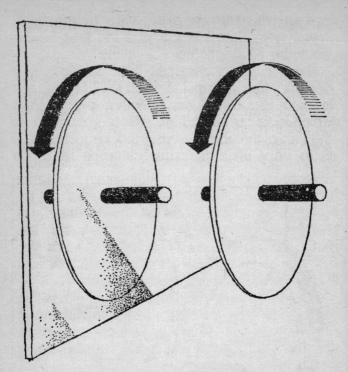

Spin a wheel in front of a mirror. The wheel may be coming toward you, yet the mirror shows it is going the opposite direction. You might try turning the wheel parallel to the mirror. Since you are behind it, it seems to be turning just the way you would expect it to.

Apart from looking at yourself in photographs you can see yourself as others see you by looking into two mirrors placed at right angles to each other. This way you get two reflections and therefore two reversals. Then try to touch your right ear while looking at yourself!

# Can you tell what someone is saying without hearing them?

Next time you watch television, lower the sound and just watch the picture. What are the people on the screen saying? You may not be able to tell, but there are some people who can.

Lip readers are people who have practiced watching the movements of other people's mouths. They learn what is being said by seeing only. Deaf people need to do this and can be taught. It is possible for a lip reader to tell what is being said by people on the opposite side of the room. If a lip reader had binoculars, he or she could watch people talking a great distance away and know all about their conversation.

Also, lip readers can tell if a silent film is run backwards. If you saw a silent film running in reverse, you would have to rely on other clues such as a clock or moving to tell that something was wrong.

# How high are the clouds?

Look at the sky when the weather is clear, when it is cloudy, and when it is rainy. The clouds you see not only look different; they *are* different. Different types of clouds form the higher up the tiny droplets of water, or clouds, are seen in the sky.

Big, white, fluffy, separate clouds are called *cumulus* clouds. They are quite low, only about 2,000 feet high, and not very thick.

With rising air pushing them up, they can become much thicker and begin to look black. They are turning into storm clouds. *Cumulo-nimbus* is the name given to them. They can be very tall, measuring from 1,500 to 25,000 feet. These black and white storm clouds can produce thunderstorms.

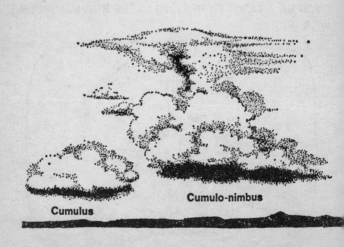

Cumulo-nimbus

Cumulus

*Stratus* clouds are higher than cumulus clouds and start about 3,000 feet up. The lower stratus clouds are like sheets of gray. When they line the sky, the day often looks miserable and rain may fall.

Higher stratus clouds, called *alto-stratus*, give the sky a "watery" look.

*Cirrus* clouds, the highest of all, float between 20,000 and 40,000 feet above the earth. They are made of ice crystals because it is so cold that high up. Depending on the winds and their height, cirrus clouds can look wispy and thin. Some people call this a mare's tail sky.

*Cirro-stratus* clouds, which may be 30,000 feet high, can create a halo effect around the sun.

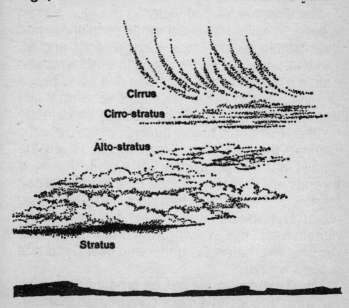

Cirrus

Cirro-stratus

Alto-stratus

Stratus

# How are velvet and satin made?

You might think that velvet and satin are materials, just like cotton, wool, and nylon. Instead, velvet and satin describe the way material is woven. Velvet may be made of cotton or rayon, but it is woven in a velvet weave. This is also true for a satin weave.

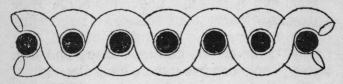

**plain weave**

The simplest kind of weaving is called a plain weave. In a plain weave threads pass under and over thread which cross them at right angles. Cloth is woven using very long threads wrapped onto a roller and unrolled a little at a time. These are the *warp* threads. They look somewhat like the strings of a harp. Every second thread may be lifted to make a tunnel through which a shuttle carrying the *weft* thread can travel. When the shuttle has gone through the tunnel, the warp threads are reversed. Those that were lifted can be dropped, and those that were dropped can be lifted. The shuttle passes back in the opposite direction and the weaving continues. In this way the shuttle creates the under and over pattern of a plain weave.

Many more weaves can be produced by lifting the warp threads in a more complicated manner.

In a satin weave the surface you see has very long threads travelling in one direction. These weft threads lie on the surface for ¼ of an inch or more and then dive down into the cloth. This gives the surface a silky look.

**satin weave**

Velvet is another complicated weave. It starts as a very thick cloth. After weaving, the cloth is cut in half. This leaves two pieces of material. The cut threads stand up just like very fine animal fur!

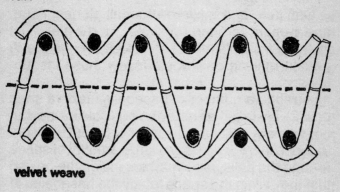

**velvet weave**

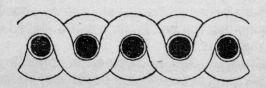

# How do you make concrete?

If you have ever seen concrete being poured, you might think that it is a strange, gray mush that magically becomes hard. Making concrete, though, is not really very mysterious.

Concrete is a mixture of small stones, sand, and cement (ground up stone), and water. Just imagine a simple model of a block of concrete. A person making one would follow these instructions:
1) Arrange a number of baseballs inside a shoe box. 2) Try to get as many as possible inside, but not so many that the lid could not be put back on. 3) Since there is actually a large amount of space around the balls, drop marbles inside the box so that they fill up the space left by the baseballs. 4) Pour little ball bearings over the marbles and baseballs because there is still some space left. 5) Notice that the box is almost 100% filled with solid materials.

The gravel, sand, and cement of concrete can be compared in size to the baseballs, marbles, ball bearings of this model. Builders mix the ingredients with water. The water helps the pieces of gravel, sand, and cement to slide over each other and leave no air space. All of these materials fill up the space of a block of concrete. Concrete gets hard when all the mixing water has dried out. The reason concrete becomes hard is that the powdered, or ground up stone chemically changes to a new substance which binds the other materials together as the whole block dries.

You know that concrete is hard, but it is hard in a special way. A tall concrete column can support a very heavy weight. Builders make concrete stronger by adding steel bars if they know that it will have to take a lot of stress.

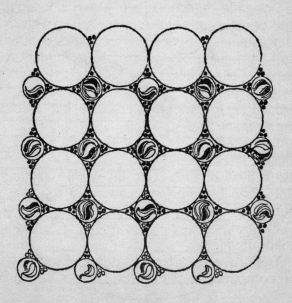

# How do you draw an ellipse?

An ellipse looks like a circle that has been "squashed." To understand how an ellipse is made, you must first look at how a circle can be drawn. If you don't have a compass, you still make an ellipse easily. Stick a pin into drawing paper. Attach a string to it and to a pencil. Stretch the string and draw around the pin. If you have held the pencil straight, all the points on the line you have drawn will be the same distance from the pin. That is what a circle is — the set of points that are equally far apart from a point.

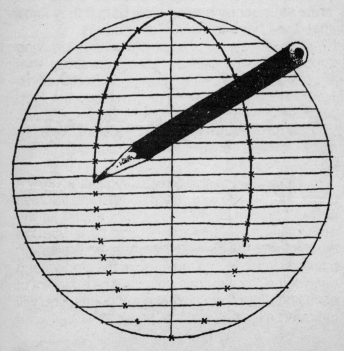

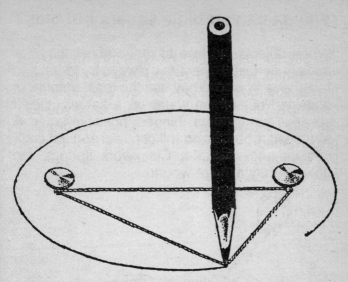

To make an ellipse stick two pins in drawing paper. Make a loop of thread or string that passes over the pins and still has some slack. Take up the slack with a pencil. Keep the loop pulled tight and the pencil straight as you draw. You will have drawn an ellipse. Like the circle, an ellipse curves, but it moves about two center points, not just one.

Another way to draw an ellipse is to first draw a circle. Then make a series of parallel lines across it. Next, draw a single line at right angles to the parallel lines. This line must also pass through the center of the circle. Now measure the length between this line and the edge of the circle along each of the parallel lines, marking the midpoint of each line. If you join all these midpoints, you will make an ellipse.

# Why can't you blow square bubbles?

When objects are free to move about they be-
have in certain ways. They always try to get into
the shape in which they use the least amount of
energy. Pour a little water on a flat surface. It
spreads out into the thinnest possible layer. A
stretched rubber band will contract and get back
into its original state. Clockwork springs run
down if they are not wound.

Soap bubbles, just like water molecules have surface tension. This skin like surface creates the shape of the bubble. A soap film will have the least energy needed to hold it together when the space it encloses is the greatest. A circle is the two-dimensional shape that encloses the biggest area. The sphere, or the round bubble that you always get when you blow soap bubbles, takes up the largest amount of space for its surface area. So, it is the shape that needs the least energy.

Suppose a square bubble were blown — which never could happen! What do you think would happen? It would be difficult for the corners to stay sharp. Eventually they would curve and the bubble would become a round sphere again.

# Why does a faucet drip?

Go to your kitchen and turn on the water. Then gradually turn it off. The water turns from a steady flow to a narrow stream that begins to break into beads a few inches below the faucet. As the faucet is shut off more, the stream slows immediately. It is possible to adjust the tap so that one drop falls every few seconds or even minutes.

Drops or beads are formed because the water has surface tension. The molecules of water attract one another and form a skin. This skin is strong enough to act as a bag whose shape is a sphere. Water droplets become spheres for the same reason that soap bubbles are spheres. A sphere has the minimum surface area for its volume. A water droplet in a sphere shape needs the least amount of energy to stay together.

When a drop attached to a faucet has reached a certain size, its surface tension can no longer hold its weight. It begins to fall. Because of the extra weight of the droplets, they change into ellipse shapes to round shapes and back again.

Another thing is responsible for a faucet drip. Inside the faucet is a *washer* made of rubber or some other bendable material. A washer can be pressed on the opening that causes the water to flow. As the washer seals this opening, less and less water can pass. The flow turns into a trickle until nothing is left at all. If a faucet drips when it is supposed to be off, the washer has probably been worn down.

# What happens in an eclipse?

You certainly know about something that always seems to follow you — your shadow. Think about it for a minute. When is a shadow formed? You cannot have a shadow in complete darkness. You need light to have a shadow. Also, you must be between the light and the wall, floor, or ground that the shadow will fall on. A shadow will not be cast if the light is between you and the other surface. When the light hits you at one angle, your shadow will have a certain look — it may be long and in front of you. At a different angle, your shadow will change — it may be short and be behind you.

Eclipses are shadows that occur when the sun, moon, and earth are in line with one another. Like the light source that makes your shadow, the sun must be one of the outer objects.

When the earth is in the center, it can shade all

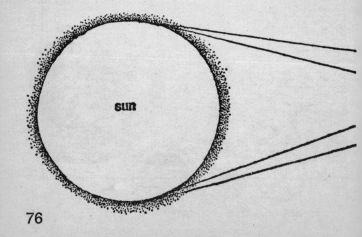

sun

or part of the moon. You can then see the round shadow of the earth pass across the moon in a matter of minutes.

Spectacular eclipses occur when the sun, moon, and earth are in line with the moon in the center. With the moon exactly in line between sun and earth, it is just possible for it to block out the sun's rays entirely. This is called a *total* eclipse and happens in a particular place one or two times in three centuries. The C area in the illustration is where a total eclipse is taking place. The B area is the *partial* eclipse area, where the sun's rays are not entirely blocked out.

A total eclipse can be a frightening experience, just as if night suddenly fell without any twilight. Long ago, before people knew about these things, they thought that a total eclipse meant the end of the world.

Eclipses can be predicted. Scientists can figure out when they will pass. Almanacs and newspapers tell when an eclipse will occur in your area.

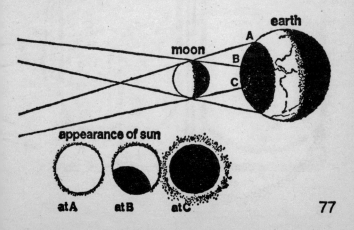

appearance of sun

at A    at B    at C

# How does a fire extinguisher work?

You see fire extinguishers frequently in your school and other places. Have you ever wondered how they work? Putting out a fire makes you think of firemen's hoses and pumping water. But, fire extinguishers work in a different way.

To understand how one kind of fire extinguisher works, you must know how fire burns. There must be oxygen for a fire to stay lit. If all the oxygen is gone, then a fire can no longer burn.

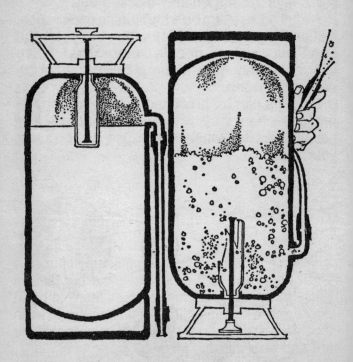

When you trigger a fire extinguisher, it forces a jet of foam to shoot out. When the bubbles of foam hit the fire, the heat causes them to burst and a gas is released. This replaces the oxygen that the fire needs to stay alive. It "smothers" the fire and puts it out.

# Why does a heap of grass cuttings get hot in the middle?

If you put your hand in a heap of grass cuttings about an hour after the lawn has been mowed, you will find that their temperature is very much higher than the air outside. If you test it again later, it may be very hot, so beware!

What is happening is that the grass has already begun to rot and produce heat. The grass in the middle of the pile feels hotter than the outside grass because the heat inside is trapped.

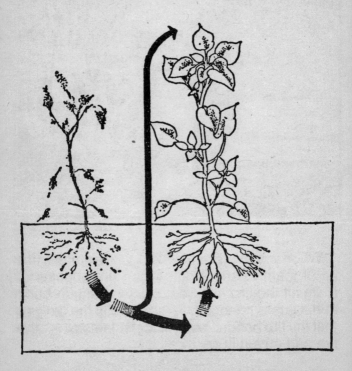

The heat of the outer grass can escape more easily into the surrounding air.

Like grass, other living things decay once they have died. Chemical changes begin, and these chemical changes produce heat. The parts that made up the whole thing — plant or animal — break down. That is not the end of them, though. The parts get recycled into useful materials that help soil be fertile and plants to grow.

Even if a plant is eaten by an animal, the animal's waste material is full of things needed to make plants grow. What is more, they are even more concentrated than they were in the growing plant. That is why gardeners find manure to be such good fertilizer.

# How can a wine glass be broken by a musical note?

Perhaps you have seen on television a scene in which a singer breaks a wine glass when she reaches a high note. "Trick photography," you may say. But, it is not so. It can really happen.

Sound does special things to objects as it bumps into them and passes through them. Depending on how fast the sound vibrates, it

can make particular kinds of objects move back and forth. When an object is pushed by sound and continues to be pushed so that it exaggerates its natural rhythm, *resonance* occurs.

Hard substances have what is called *frequency*. Frequency describes rhythms. The resonant frequency of glass depends on the materials it is made of, its thickness, and its size. Glass has a high resonant frequency, which means that only a very high sound can break glass.

No musical instrument or human voice can produce a pure note. Pianos and violins and singers make sounds that are mixtures of a certain note plus sounds of much higher frequencies. Look at the singer in the illustration. Female singers' top notes are claimed to be more than the resonant frequency of glass. The right combination of them are also strong enough to break certain kinds of glass, like delicate wine glasses.

# How does a jet engine work?

If someone told you that a jet engine is like a balloon, you would probably say "Ridiculous!" But, you would be wrong.

Blow up a balloon; let go of it; feel the air coming from it. Compare that to the direction that the balloon begins to move. The air blows one way, the balloon goes in the opposite way. You can repeat this many times. It will always happen in this manner.

This gives you an idea how rockets work. The hot gases shooting out of a rocket move in one direction. The rocket moves in the opposite direction. A balloon which has escaping air coming from it is very much like a rocket. There is no difference, really, except that a rocket has hot gases coming from it rather than cold air.

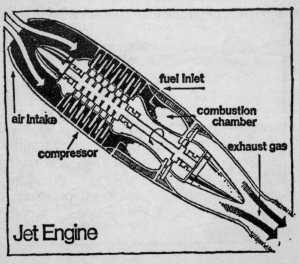

Jet Engine

fuel inlet

combustion chamber

air intake

exhaust gas

compressor

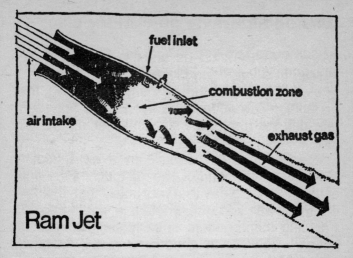

## Ram Jet

The jet engine obviously is more complicated than a balloon, or rocket. This is because it also has an engine in it. The jet engine throws out air and waste products from the burned fuel in one direction, so that it can move in the other one. This goes on all the time the engine runs.

Four things happen to make a jet engine go:
1. Air is drawn into a chamber.
2. It is pressed down and fuel is added.
3. Fuel is burned and the air expands.
4. Air is forced out along with waste products.

In a turbojet, air is drawn in by fan blades which are also used to compress it, or press against it.

The simplest jet engine of all is a lot like a metal tube. Where the pipe swells out, pressure increases, and where it narrows, pressure decreases. This type of engine must be given a flying start.

# Why do old trains go clickety-clack?

When a metal such as steel is heated, it expands. In a very long piece of metal, a railroad track, for example, that is many yards long, the expansion can actually be seen. On a hot summer day the track may stretch a half an inch or more.

Imagine that the railway lines were laid in place so that the end of one rail touched the end of the next. On a day that was hotter than the day the track was laid, the whole line would buckle. Knowing this, builders of early steam railroads left gaps between neighboring tracks. If you have ever ridden on an antique locomotive, you probably heard and felt the clickety-clack the train made as it went over the expansion joints.

Modern railroads do not bump because their tracks are made of a continuous steel bar. It does not buckle on a hot day or split on a cold one. Builders now use a special technique. When a rail is laid, they heat it to a temperature higher than that of the hottest day. While it is still hot, they bond the rail to the sleepers, the part that lies on the ground.

# Does the earth have a crust?

The word *crust* usually describes the outside of a loaf of bread, a pie, or a cheese. So the earth's crust is simply the outside of the earth. But how thick is it, and what substance does it contain?

Scientists believe that the center of the earth is a solid surrounded by a thick layer of a very hot liquid. The outside limits of this liquid form a ball of about 2,200 miles in diameter. This is surrounded by a very thick layer — about 1,800 miles — of a half-solid, half-liquid called the *mantle*, that can flow and change its shape. Outside comes the *crust*, as thin in comparison to the earth's diameter as the thinnest crust of a loaf. The earth's crust varies in thickness from about 3 to 20 miles.

Even the crust itself can be divided into two layers. The inner layer is known as the **Sima** because the main substance that makes it up are **SI**licon and **MA**gnesium. The outer layer is named **Sial**, since it is mostly **SI**licon and **AL**uminum. But this layer also contains all the other minerals that give us metal and thousands of other chemicals.

The sima layer is made up mostly of basalt. This is a heavy, dark-colored rock. Many lavas are made up of basalt. Basalt is found mainly in the oceans. Granite floats on top of basalt. It is a lighter colored rock. Most of the world's continents are made up mostly of granite.

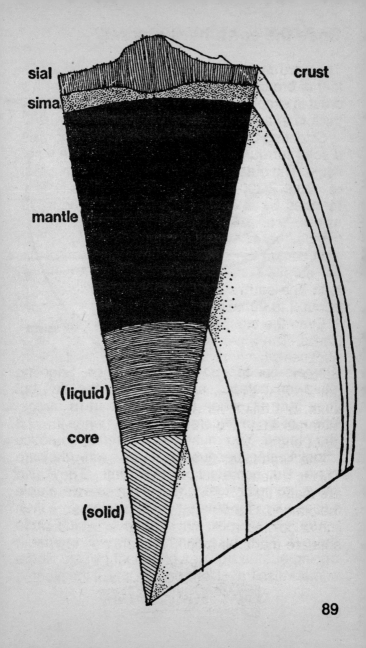

sial

sima

mantle

(liquid)

core

(solid)

crust

# Is a comet a shooting star?

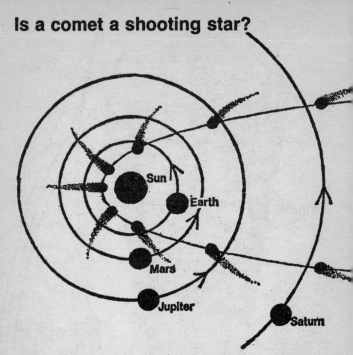

Comets speed through outer space. Shooting stars, or meteors, streak through the sky, but they burn up when they reach earth's atmosphere of air, or become meteorites when they hit the ground. You must watch carefully to notice shooting stars because, quick as a wink, they are gone. But comets take their time. They also move incredibly fast, but sometimes we are able to see them for several days, or nights.

Comets are also unlike planets which circle the sun. They take enormous swings in space, tracing out the outlines of a giant ellipse. Some comets also travel farther than any of the planets

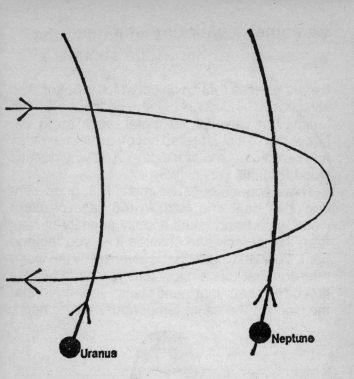

Uranus

Neptune

in their huge orbits.

One famous comet, Halley's Comet, orbits the sun every 76 years. Some comets appear once every hundred years or so; others more often; and some were last seen hundreds of years ago!

Comets are small objects compared with the earth. They are made up of frozen gas, dust, and pieces of ice. They look as if they have a fiery tail. When comets approach the sun, their tails are behind them, but when they speed away, their tails seem to lead the way. Their tails always point away from the sun.

## Why does metal feel so cold in the winter and so hot in the summer?

It makes sense that an object which is hotter than your body (98.6 degrees) should feel hot to the touch. But why should metal, such as in the bodywork of a car, feel so hot on a summer's day and so cold on a winter's day? And why doesn't wood feel this way?

This happens because metal is a good conductor of heat and cold. In the case of warm wood, your hand takes a small quantity of heat from the surface and absorbs it — you feel the heat. Very little extra heat is given off by the wood after the first touch. Now that you have felt the first bit of heat, your hand "tells" your brain that the wood is the same temperature as the hand.

The amount of heat is so small that a rise in temperature is hardly noticed. If you touch hot metal, more and more heat pours into your hand from deep in the metal. On a cold day the opposite happens. Metal conducts the heat away from the hand, so it feels very cold.

In touching the hot and cold metal, your hands are giving you a clear message. Sometimes your hands can play tricks on you, just as your eyes can deceive you. Your hands tend to "remember" what they have felt in the past and compare it with the present. Get bowls of hot, cold, and warm water. Put your right hand in the hot water and your left hand in the cold water. Then quickly put both hands in the warm water. How do they feel? The hand from the hot bowl will feel cold and the one from the cold bowl will feel hot!

# What makes a sonic boom?

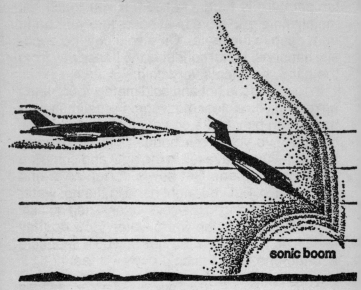

sonic boom

Have you ever heard a tremendous, thunder-like sound in the sky even when there was no storm? Have you wondered what could make such a noise?

Nowadays, jet planes travel at amazing speeds. Some, such as the Concorde jet, can zoom faster than the speed of sound. These aircraft are called *supersonic*. Sonic means having to do with sound. They are also called SST's, or super-sonic transports.

As they fly through the sky, jets make huge amounts of noise. The noise travels through the air in all directions as sound waves. The waves